Dinosaurs
Swimming Giants

by Monica Hughes

Consultant: Dougal Dixon

ticktock

Copyright © **ticktock Entertainment Ltd 2007**
First published in Great Britain in 2007 by **ticktock Media Ltd.,**
Unit 2, Orchard Business Centre, North Farm Road, Tunbridge Wells, Kent TN2 3XF

We would like to thank: Shirley Bickler and Suzanne Baker

ISBN 978 1 84696 605 7 pbk
Printed in China

Picture credits
t=top, b=bottom, c=centre, l-left, r=right, OFC= outside front cover
John Alston: 5b; Simon Mendez: 1, 4-5, 8-9, 12-13, 19, 20-21, 22t, 22b; Luis Rey: 1,
6, 14-15, 16-17, 23t, 23b; Shutterstock: 7t, 8, 10-11, 14, 17t, 18, 23c.

CONTENTS

Swimming creatures

There were lots of swimming creatures at the time of the dinosaurs.

Some were big and some were small.

They were all good at swimming.

Ceresiosaurus
ser-ee-see-o-sor-us

Many of the creatures had sharp teeth to catch fish.

Placodus

This is Placodus. It was about two metres long.

Placodus walked along the sea bed hunting for shellfish.

It had four legs and a long tail. It also had webbed feet.

Webbed feet

Newt

It looked like a giant newt.

Short head

Placodus
plak-o-dus

Tail

A giant sea creature

This swimming giant was 15 metres long.

It had a short neck and a long head.

It had sharp teeth.

Kronosaurus
kroh-no-sor-us

Octopus

It ate octopus and giant squid.

What a long neck!

This swimming creature was very big.

Its neck was longer than its body.

It had a small head.

Elasmosaurus
ee-las-mo-sor-us

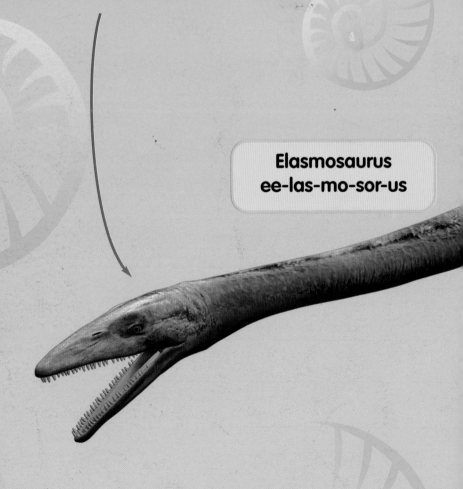

It had a short tail.

It had long legs like paddles.

On land and in the sea

This creature was three metres long.

It had a long head and lots of sharp teeth.

Nothosaurus
noth-o-sor-us

This animal sometimes went
on land, but most of the time
it swam in the sea.

It had webbed feet
to help it to swim.

Webbed feet

Is it a snake or a turtle?

This creature had a long neck
and long pointed teeth.

Fish

It ate fish and squid.

It looked like a cross between a snake and a turtle.

Cryptoclidus
crip-tow-cly-dus

Fish-lizard

This swimming creature was as big as a dolphin.

Its name means 'fish-lizard'.

Ichthyosaurus
ick-thee-o-sor-us

Squid

Eye

It ate fish and squid.

Mouth

A huge sea monster

Look at Shonisaurus. This creature was more than 15 metres long.

It was as big as a whale.

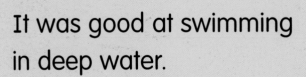
Whale

It was good at swimming in deep water.

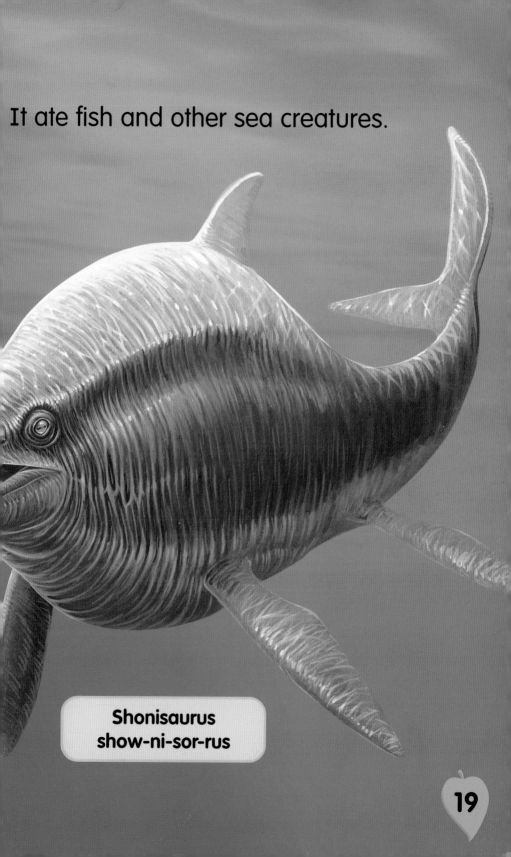

It ate fish and other sea creatures.

Shonisaurus
show-ni-sor-rus

What a long creature!

This swimming creature had a long body and a flat tail.

It had a long nose and very sharp teeth.

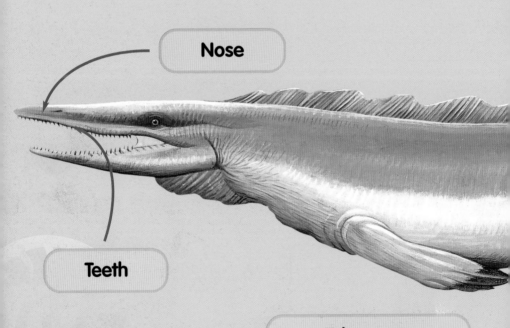

Nose

Teeth

Tylosaurus
tie-low-sor-us

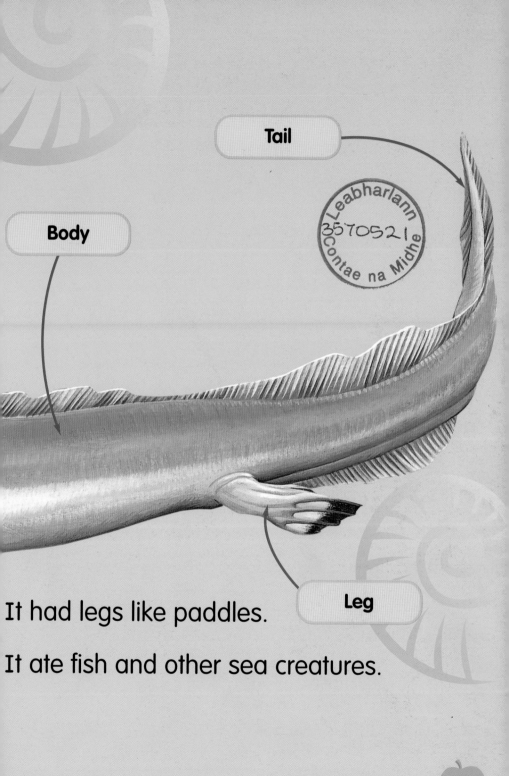

Tail

Body

Leg

It had legs like paddles.

It ate fish and other sea creatures.

Thinking and talking about swimming giants

Which swimming creature looked like a giant newt?

Which swimming creature sometimes went on land?

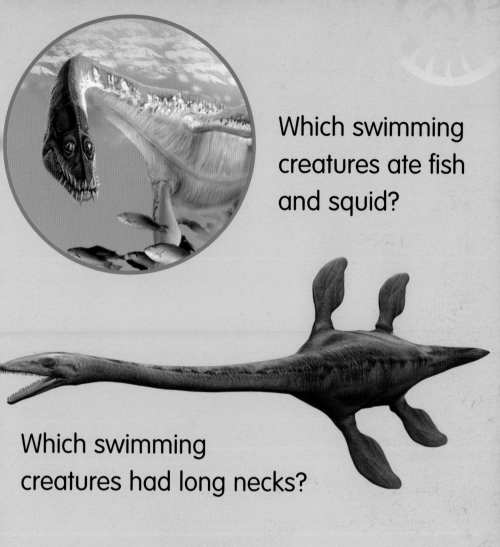

Which swimming
creatures ate fish
and squid?

Which swimming
creatures had long necks?

What does
Ichthyosaurus
mean?

Activities

What did you think of this book?

 Brilliant **Good** **OK**

Which page did you like best? Why?

• • • • • • • • • • • • •

Which of these ate fish and squid?

Tylosaurus • Icthyosaurus • Cryptoclidus

• • • • • • • • • • • •

Invent a giant swimming creature. Give it a long neck, long jaws, sharp teeth and flippers like paddles. Give it a name.

• • • • • • • • • • • •

Who is the author of this book?
Have you read *Dinosaur World Flying Giants* by the same author?